Aditi and her Friends on their 10th adventure

Monkeyji and the Word Eater

Aditi and her Friends on their **10**th adventure

Monkeyji and the Word Eater

Suniti Namjoshi

pictures
Proiti Roy

Tulika

Monkeyji and the Word Eater (English)

ISBN 978-81-8146-779-9

First published in India, 2009
Reprinted 2013

Published by
Tulika Publishers, 24/1 Ganapathy Colony Third Street, Teynampet, Chennai 600 018, India
email tulikabooks@vsnl.com *website* www.tulikabooks.com

Printed and bound at
the ind-com press, 393 Velachery Main Road, Vijaynagar, Velachery, Chennai 600 042, India

For

Christine Mary

who was hurt as a child,

but who survived, and is lovely.

THE FOUR ADVENTURERS

Aditi is a brave little girl, who hates fighting, but can wield the Sword of Courage when necessary. She loves the other three adventurers, the two dragons and her grandparents more than anything in the world.

Beautiful Ele the Beautiful Elephant tries hard to be as logical as Siril. Like Goldie she is immensely strong and warm-hearted.

Siril the ant loves maps and long words and his friends. He sometimes wishes he wasn't quite so small.

The One-eyed Monkey or **Monkeyji** is older than the others and so tries hard to be wise and sensible.

THE TWO DRAGONS

Goldie, a fire-breathing sea dragon, and **Opal**, a beautiful and gentle river dragon, fly the adventurers everywhere because they are their friends. They usually live on an island with the Island Sage.

OTHER CHARACTERS

Aditi's grandparents are the rulers of a small kingdom in western India. They have given Aditi and her friends the Sword of Courage, a cloak of invisibility and some magic clay in order to help them protect themselves. The four adventurers live with them.

The Three Sages are three wise sisters for whom the adventurers sometimes run errands. The adventurers can turn to them for help. The Island Sage lives on an island off the west coast of India and is surrounded by lionesses and their cubs. The Marine Sage lives on the Great Barrier Reef off the coast of Australia, and the Techno Sage lives on a lake in Canada.

Gardy is one of the lion cubs who lives with the Island Sage. He accompanied the adventurers when they had to deliver a message to the Techno Sage, and the adventurers accompanied him when he went to the City of Lions.

Grendel lives with his mother on the south-west coast of England. His mother is a friend of Aditi's grandmother. He and the adventurers are good friends.

Otto, Grendel's cousin, is a very clever boy who gets bullied at school. In order to fight back he learns how to make words disappear.

It is said that there were eight hills in the Hong Kong area, each of which was a Dragon; the Ninth Dragon was the Emperor himself, a Golden Dragon.

1

The Black and White Butterflies

It was Aditi who first noticed them. The black and white butterflies had settled on each side of Beautiful's head like a pair of earrings. At first she thought that they were earrings and was about to say to the elephant how pretty they were. She looked at them more closely and saw that the black marks on their white wings were letters of the alphabet, and that the letters kept changing. Before she could exclaim, the elephant pushed her away gently. "Wait," she said. "The butterflies are trying to tell me something." It was clear that Beautiful was concentrating hard. Aditi and the One-eyed Monkey and Siril the Ant, who was perched on Aditi's shoulder, waited patiently. As they watched Siril realised that the letters on the butterflies' wings were making complete words. He pointed this out to Aditi and Monkeyji in great excitement. They immediately stationed themselves on either side of Beautiful, and read out whatever they could decipher.

"DANGER," Aditi murmured. "I think I've seen that word twice. And KING."

"No, it's KONG. And EATING or EAT? EAT something?

I've seen something with EAT in it once or twice," Monkeyji added.

Suddenly the two butterflies opened and closed their wings twice. The letters fell away. Their wings turned snow white, then black and then the butterflies disappeared altogether. They didn't rise into the air and fly away, they just disappeared. Aditi, Siril and Monkeyji waited for Beautiful to say something, but she seemed dazed and stood there without saying a word.

At last Siril lost patience. "Aren't you going to tell us what the butterflies told you?" he said to Beautiful.

Beautiful turned towards him. "Shsh," she said. "It's dangerous to speak. And don't even mention them, those, I mean the ones..."

"Do you mean the butterflies?" asked Monkeyji thinking that for a moment Beautiful couldn't remember what they were called.

"Oh hush!" cried Beautiful. She was clearly distressed. "You mustn't even mention them."

"Why not?" asked Aditi.

"Because," said Beautiful looking at the others solemnly, "they'll get eaten."

"By whom?" asked Siril in astonishment.

"Shsh. Can't talk here," Beautiful told him. "We might be overheard."

Beautiful rolled her eyes upwards. When the others looked up all that they could see was an ordinary crow sitting peacefully on one of the branches of the banyan tree.

"He might be a spy," Beautiful whispered to the others. "Let's move away."

The others looked at the crow doubtfully. The crow was paying no attention to them at all. They followed Beautiful into a large room outside the house in which Aditi's grandparents lived. Beautiful looked around cautiously.

"Those butterflies are a new type of email message," she began.

"Do you mean that it's now possible to send three-dimensional images instead of just two-dimensional ones?" Siril asked. "I knew that work was being done to make that possible. Were they digital butterflies?"

Beautiful nodded. "I think so. They had been sent with a message for all of us, but they happened to settle on my head, and when they began talking to each other, I overheard them. Once they realised I could hear them, they gave me the message, because they weren't quite sure how long they would last."

"Yes, they did disappear quite suddenly, didn't they?" the One-eyed Monkey murmured. "Who was the message from and what did it say?"

"The message was from Grendel, Monkeyji," Beautiful replied. "He wants us to go to Hong Kong and save his cousin, who has become a Word Eater and calls himself King of the Crows. He may begin terrorising the city, and then everyone in the city will be out to get him."

"Are we supposed to save the Word Eater, whoever he is, or the city?" asked Monkeyji, puzzled.

"What's a Word Eater?" asked Siril.

"What exactly is this Word Eater doing? And why is he doing it?" asked Aditi.

"I think we're supposed to save the Word Eater and the city," Beautiful said to Monkeyji.

She turned to Siril. "I don't know what a Word Eater is either," she told him. "But it must be someone who swallows words, don't you think?"

And finally she turned to Aditi. "I've forgotten your question," she mumbled.

Aditi smiled. "I'm sorry," she said. "We've all been firing questions at you. Why didn't Grendel just send an ordinary email and explain everything?"

"He has. He did. We should get it soon. He thought the butterflies would be quicker and that we would like them. "

"Well, I'll check whether an email has arrived," said Siril turning away.

"Yes, do. But whether it has arrived or not, we have to leave at once. Grendel says it's an EMERGENCY," Beautiful told him.

The others looked at Beautiful and she looked back at them worriedly. It was clear that she was entirely serious.

Monkeyji sighed. She was gradually becoming more and more reluctant to travel, but Grendel was an old friend. They had met him and his mother when they had travelled to the southwest coast of England. Perhaps they would be coming to Hong Kong too? She cheered up at the thought. "Will Grendel and his mother be joining us?"

Beautiful shook her head. "They can't. Grendel's mother and her sister are both poorly. The Word Eater is her sister's son. That's why Grendel is asking us to please go and sort things out. He's worried about what his cousin has been getting up to."

The others nodded. It was a strange account, but it was beginning to make sense. They began to make preparations for the journey to Hong Kong. Siril and Aditi went to the computer to check for incoming emails and to send a message to the two dragons, Goldie and Opal, asking whether they would be willing to fly them to Hong Kong. The dragons were always ready for an adventure and had never refused, and so Monkeyji and Beautiful didn't wait for a reply. Beautiful hauled out the howdah, which would be strapped to Goldie's back, and she and Monkeyji began to pack. They decided to take the Sword of Courage, the cloak of invisibility, Sirl's matchbox with the magic clay, and a knapsack containing a couple of ointments for making them larger or smaller, and another jar of ointment for healing cuts and bruises. They also packed some food and water, and Beautiful threw in a couple of extra sacks of peanuts just in case they were needed.

2

Cousin Otto

Monkeyji and Beautiful had barely finished packing when Goldie and Opal appeared high overhead and Siril and Aditi emerged from the house. Aditi had Grendel's email in her hand and was waving it. Siril was carrying a large pouch. He gave it to Monkeyji.

"Please pack it carefully with the other things in the knapsack," he asked.

"What is it?" Beautiful wanted to know.

Siril hesitated, then he opened the pouch and showed them what was inside it. "It's my word-hoard," he explained. "I have a feeling it might come in useful." The pouch contained dozens of silver balls of different sizes. Siril had written his favourite long words on pieces of silver paper and rolled up the silver paper into balls.

Beautiful and Monkeyji stared at them. "They're pretty," Monkeyji said at last.

"Yes," agreed Beautiful. "But how do you know which word is which?"

"Oh, I don't," answered Siril. "From the size of the ball I

can only judge the length of the word. The longer they are the better, though not always. Look this one here is fairly large, it's probably PALINDROME." He opened up the ball and sure enough that was the word written inside.

Monkeyji stared at Siril and shook her head. Sometimes he did some strange things, but he usually had a reason for whatever he did.

Just then Goldie and Opal landed. Gardy, the youngest lion cub, was clinging to Goldie's neck. He seemed reluctant to climb down.

Aditi looked at the cub in surprise. "Hello," she called. "What are you doing here?"

"He stowed away by hanging on to my tail," Goldie replied. "When I realised it, I stopped and let him climb up to my neck where it's safer. It was too late to turn back. From your email we knew you were in a hurry."

Gardy climbed down slowly. The others looked at him. "Well, you'll just have to stay here," Monkeyji said severely.

Gardy hung his head. "I'm sorry for stowing away, Monkeyji," he said. "I heard Goldie and Opal say something about a Word Eater, and I wanted to come and help. I brought you my word-hoard — in case it might be useful." He handed Monkeyji a pouch which was very similar to Siril's. "You could use it as bait perhaps?" he said hopefully.

Monkeyji and the others couldn't help smiling and Siril took pity on him. "If he promises to be good and to do exactly what I say, might he be allowed to come with us please?" he asked the others. "I will be responsible for him. And anyway, don't you remember how well he managed things when we all went to the City of Lions?"

Monkeyji looked at the two of them with their word-hoards stashed in pouches, then she looked at Aditi and Beautiful to see how they felt. It was clear they didn't mind. "Yes, he can come," she said. "When we went to see the Techno Sage, he was the Guardian of the Time Jewels, this time he can be the Guardian of the Word-Hoards." And with that she tied the two pouches around Gardy's neck. Gardy was so pleased that he squirmed and wriggled and turned a somersault and found that he couldn't say a word.

They delayed no further. They took leave of Aditi's grandparents, and the four adventurers crowded into the howdah on Goldie's back. Gardy clung to Opal's neck to keep her company. The dragons rose in the air and set off eastwards. Aditi began to read Grendel's message. Opal tried flying close to Goldie in order to hear what Aditi was saying, but the wind kept snatching the words away. And it was clear from the way Goldie kept turning his head that he couldn't hear properly either. Trying to fly and listen at the same time was too dangerous, Opal decided. "Brief Goldie and me later," she called out to Aditi,

as she moved away to a safe distance. Goldie too gave up trying to hear what was being said, but the others listened intently to Grendel's email as Aditi read it aloud:

> *"My cousin, Otto, really isn't a bad chap. He used to like to be on his own and spend his time thinking. He wasn't very sociable. So he was sent to a boarding school in Hong Kong to teach him to get on with other boys. Well, as you know, my mother and I have greenish skins, and so has my cousin, Otto. The other boys thought this strange and began to tease him. And he made matters worse by being much cleverer than them and not bothering to hide it. Nor did he try to make friends with any of them. He had always been a loner and that's the way he liked it. But the other boys wouldn't leave him alone. The name-calling got worse. Cabbagehead, Broccoliboy — that sort of thing. I know about this, because he wrote to me. I told him to ignore the bullies, and to make friends with some of the other boys. But he wouldn't.*
>
> *One day he emailed me saying that the name-calling had stopped. He had found a way of snatching the words as they came out of the boys' mouths. Once he'd grabbed a word, he wrote to me triumphantly, the word just disappeared. Well, I didn't know whether to believe him or not. My cousin Otto has always had exceptional mental powers. Anyway, I stopped worrying about him. For a while there were no more emails from him and I decided*

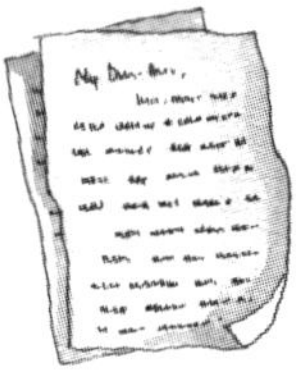

that no news was good news. But lately my emails to him have been bouncing. And when his mother tried to phone his school, the operator didn't seem to know what she was talking about. And she says her emails to the school have also bounced.

I would go myself to find out what's happening, but both my aunt and my mother are unwell and I don't want to leave them. If you would go to Hong Kong, please, and check up on Otto, both my mother and I would be extremely grateful. We send our regards to Aditi's grandparents and our thanks to you in advance.

As I said before, Otto isn't really a bad chap, but he's only little and I'm afraid both for him as well as because of him. He may not realise how much destruction he can cause.

Your friend,

Grendel

PS: Otto's mum has arranged for you to stay on an empty boat called *The Stranger* which is moored opposite the Aberdeen section of the city. It belongs to a friend of hers whose son goes to the same school as Otto."

When Aditi finished reading, everyone except Monkeyji started talking at once.

"Do you think he's made the school disappear?" Beautiful wondered.

"He could be dangerous," Aditi murmured.

"What about the crows?" Siril demanded.

"Oh, I know about the crows," Beautiful told him. "That's what the butterflies were grumbling about to each other from either side of my head. It turns out that when the Word Eater tried to eat the bad words the boys called him, they stuck in his throat, so he chucked them in the flower beds in the garden in his school. Some crows who were sitting on the rooftops thought he was throwing them breadcrumbs. They flew down and scoffed them up like chips or peanuts. The crows really liked them. They keep hoping he'll throw them a few more words. They call him Otto the Word Eater, King of the Crows. Oh, and they've developed a taste for digital butterflies. That's why the butterflies really hate crows."

Beautiful stopped suddenly. She had said all this so fast that she was almost out of breath.

"What happens to the words the crows eat?" Siril asked thoughtfully. "Do they disappear forever?"

"I don't know," replied Beautiful.

Monkeyji's face had suddenly become very grim. "This is much more serious than I thought," she said and her voice had a dark edge in it they had never heard before.

She leaned forward and whispered something in Goldie's ear. The dragons suddenly tripled their speed. After that there was no more talking as the wind whistled past everyone's ears. Within a couple of hours they had reached Hong Kong and the dragons had settled on the water beside the boat called *The Stranger*.

3

The Tenth Dragon

"Right," said Monkeyji as she jumped into the boat, "as soon as Opal, Goldie and Beautiful have rubbed some of the Make-Small ointment on themselves, we must hold a council of war."

"War?" asked Siril wonderingly. "Otto is only a little boy."

"He may be a very powerful little boy," replied Monkeyji. "We must find him before he does any more harm."

"Why don't we go to his school," suggested Beautiful, "and see if he's there."

"Didn't you notice," Aditi replied thoughtfully, "that Grendel didn't mention the name of his school. I don't think he knows it. I don't think anybody knows it anymore."

"You mean – ?" asked Beautiful looking at Aditi incredulously.

Aditi nodded. "I think he may have swallowed the name of the school, or at least snatched it."

Goldie and Opal had made themselves small and now climbed aboard the boat. When they saw the concern on everyone's face they asked what was the matter.

"We're looking for a small boy called Otto," Aditi told them. "We think he may be hiding in his school, but nobody knows the name of the school. Perhaps he has shut it down."

"I'll go look for him," Goldie offered even though he was tired after his long flight. "This is the city of dragons. I'll ask around. Somebody will have seen something."

And before they could stop him or tell him anything more about Otto, he had slipped off the howdah and taken off.

Monkeyji turned to the others. "Siril, you and Gardy must go into the city and look for Otto. Aditi, you and Beautiful must do the same. We'll have a better chance if we split up. It's essential to find him before Goldie does. Goldie doesn't know anything about him and may come to harm. Opal, stay with me here while I meditate and try to locate Otto. If he attempts to snatch any more words, the sudden burst of mental energy should make it easy to locate him. When I do find him, Opal and I will fly there at once. If you find him first, DO NOT TRY

TO DEAL WITH HIM. Come and get me. And if at all possible, do not say anything. Do not give him any words to snatch, especially not your own names."

Opal's instinct was to fly after Goldie and try to warn him about Otto, but she obeyed Monkeyji. They had never heard Monkeyji sound so commanding before or so urgent. Everyone did what she told them to do. Siril and Gardy and Aditi and Beautiful were set ashore and went off into the city to look for Otto. Monkeyji and Opal remained on the boat. Monkeyji sat in the bow of the boat and closed her one grey eye. She was concentrating so fiercely that Opal, who was several feet away, could feel her mental waves. Opal read Grendel's email, which Aditi had left behind for her, and settled down to wait. All around her she could pick up the murmur of dragons, but it was indistinct. She hoped it wouldn't be Goldie who found Otto first.

But it was Goldie who found Otto first. He approached the problem in a straightforward way, not realising that there was much of a problem. He saw a small red dragon perched on top of Victoria Peak, and settled down beside him. From the Peak they had a splendid view of the city. Goldie said to the young dragon that he, Goldie, was a stranger in Hong Kong and would the young dragon help him please?

"Glad to," replied the red dragon. "By the way, Sir, I have been posted here to welcome the Tenth Dragon. According to the prophecy he's expected to arrive around about this time. You wouldn't by any chance – ?"

"I'm sorry," said Goldie. "I don't know anything at all about the Tenth Dragon. I myself am looking for a small boy. Tell me, at this time of year and at this time of day, are all the schools in session here?"

"They are," replied the red dragon. "At this time of day and this time of year all the children are in their schools and hard at work."

"Thank you," said Goldie and took off. Now all he had to do was fly up and down the city until he found a school in which nobody was doing any work at all. And sure enough in the Stanley area of the city, he saw what looked like a prosperous school with large playing fields on which a few boys were wandering about. They looked as though they didn't know what they were doing or why they were there. Goldie landed in the school courtyard and looked around him. He asked one or two boys whether they knew Otto, but they just shrugged and wandered off. Then he saw a small boy, whose face had a greenish tinge, peering at him from behind a bush. He didn't look in the least bit dazed. Goldie beckoned to him and when the boy came forward, Goldie asked, "Are you Otto?"

"Why are you looking for him?" the boy countered.

"I have to pick him up and take him to Monkeyji," Goldie replied.

Otto didn't like the sound of that. He decided he had better get rid of Goldie.

"I'm Otto," he said coming closer to Goldie. "Who are you?"

"I'm Goldie," Goldie replied.

As soon as his name left the dragon's mouth, Otto snatched it out of the air and put it in his pocket. The effect was devastating. Goldie couldn't remember who he was or what he was doing there. The little boy laughed and went away. Goldie was no longer a threat to him.

Goldie walked here and there and finally settled down under a frangipani tree. Two small green dragons who lived in a well in the school gardens had been watching Goldie. They approached him slowly and bowed to him. "Please Sir, "one of them asked with extreme courtesy, "are you the Tenth Dragon?"

"I might be," replied Goldie. "Why do you ask?"

"Because your coming has been prophesied," the smaller of the two dragons told him. "Please, Sir, you must be the Tenth Dragon. You are tired after your long journey. If you come with us, we will look after you and you will be able to rest."

"That's very kind of you," Goldie replied. He was feeling tired. For all he knew he might be the Tenth Dragon, whoever that was. It would be good to rest. In a befuddled state Goldie followed the two dragons who were treating him with such deference.

4

Which School?

Otto watched Goldie leave with the two dragons and thought he would now be left alone. Just as he turned away, he saw Aditi and Beautiful coming through the school gates.

"Now what?" he muttered to himself.

Aditi and Beautiful weren't sure that they had found the right school. When they got ashore, Aditi had gone up to an official at the ferry ticket office and said very politely, "Excuse me, Sir, could you tell me please to whom that beautiful boat over there belongs?" She pointed at *The Stranger*.

"Of course," replied the official. "The boat belongs to Madame Étranger. She's a prominent citizen of Hong Kong. Everyone knows her."

"I thought so," replied Aditi. "Thank you so much, Sir. I have a message to deliver to her, but the boat seems to be deserted."

"Oh well, everybody knows her house," the official told Aditi. "It's the large brown mansion, three blocks away. You can take your message there." And he gave Aditi directions.

Aditi and Beautiful made their way through the crowded Hong Kong streets with some difficulty even though Beautiful

had applied the Make-Small ointment and was only a quarter her usual size. People kept stopping them to pet Beautiful and coo over her. They thought she was a sweet, baby elephant. Beautiful had to put up with it.

They knocked on the door of the brown mansion and when the butler opened the door, Aditi told him that they were friends of Madame Grendel and wished to see Madame Étranger please.

Madame Étranger saw them at once and greeted them warmly. "Any friends of the Grendel family are always welcomc. How are they all?"

"Well, Madame Grendel and her sister are a little poorly; but we really came to ask you if you had any news of Otto," Beautiful said to her.

"Of Otto?" said Madame Étranger. "Why, no. How is little Otto?"

"But doesn't Otto go to the same school as your son?" ventured Aditi.

"Ah no," murmured Madame Étranger. "My son is a day scholar at the – at the – why it's very strange – the name seems to have slipped my mind. It will come to me soon."

"Ah," murmured Aditi. "Well, it was nice meeting you. Thank you for seeing us. We will give the Grendel family your regards when we see them next." And with that Aditi rose to go.

"You've only just come. Won't you stay for a cup of tea at least?" Madame Étranger protested.

But Aditi was already on her way out and Beautiful was following her. "We'll come back another day if we can," Aditi called hurriedly. "Goodbye. Goodbye. Thank you so much for seeing us, and for the use of your boat."

When they got to the corner of the street, Beautiful said to Aditi, "Do you think the school is somewhere in this area?"

"I think so," replied Aditi. "After all, her son is a day scholar there."

"It's no good asking, I suppose?" Beautiful murmured hopefully.

"No," Aditi shook her head regretfully. "That's the one school nobody can remember."

The two began to search the streets near the brown mansion systematically and eventually came to a set of large iron gates.

"This could be it," Aditi whispered.

"But nobody seems to be doing anything," Beautiful objected.

"That would make sense," Aditi replied, "if nobody can remember that this is supposed to be a school. Let's go and look."

They went through the gates and began walking towards Otto.

"I think that might be Otto," Beautiful whispered.

"He looks like Grendel. Shouldn't we go back and tell Monkeyji? That's what she told us to do."

"We have to make sure it is Otto," Aditi whispered back.

They approached cautiously. "Hello," Aditi began, "could you tell us please if you are Otto or if you know where he is."

"Why do you want to know? And who are you?" Otto replied.

"I'm Beautiful," Beautiful told him.

"Huh, 'conceited' I think would be more like it," Otto retorted. "I mean, what is your name?"

Before Beautiful could blurt out that that was her name, Aditi said hurriedly, "We're friends, friends of Otto."

"Otto has no friends!" the little boy shouted. "Now I know you're lying."

"We are not lying!" Beautiful shouted back. "We are Grendel's friends."

"Look, you're wasting your time," Otto told them. "I don't want or need any friends. I tried making friends with some of the boys here even after they had called me names, but that only made matters worse."

"What happened?" asked Aditi gently, hoping to calm him down.

"Well, I thought that if I could impress them, they'd stop calling me names, so I told them that I could snatch words from the air," Otto began.

"Go on," Aditi prompted.

"They didn't believe me. They started making fun of me.

One of them went and brought the Latin Grammar and told me to eat the words in there, so that we wouldn't have to have a Latin lesson the next day."

Otto paused, and saw that Aditi and Beautiful were listening intently. "Well, I didn't particularly want to snatch Latin words, but I said I'd do a few just to show them. The only thing was, I needed someone to say the words aloud, before I could snatch them. Well, they hardly knew any Latin words. And in any case I couldn't have snatched an entire language. I'm good, but not that good. Then one boy said that I had said I could just snatch the words out of the air, and that I was a liar. I tried to explain, but they started throwing things at me and making fun of me, so I ran away and hid somewhere."

"I'm so sorry," Beautiful murmured. She was feeling extremely sorry for him.

Otto didn't like that. "You needn't be sorry," he growled. "I'm fine as I am. I don't want friends and I don't need friends."

"Everyone needs friends," Aditi protested.

"WELL, I DON'T!" Otto shouted.

"Well, we're your cousin Grendel's friends and he has sent us here in order to help you," Beautiful told him

"Don't need any help!" Otto yelled.

"Yes, you do. You've been doing a great deal of damage and mischief here. And we're here to help you to straighten things out," Aditi told him.

"Don't want your help," Otto shouted. "And if you're not

careful I'll abolish elephants and little girls as well. Just say the word. I know how to." He began to advance upon them in a threatening fashion.

Just then Gardy bounded up, with Siril riding high on his head and hanging on to his right ear.

"BACK OFF!" the cub roared. "Or I'll bite you!"

5

Word Merchants

Otto backed away from the fierce little cub. "Who are you?" he asked. "And how did you get here?"

"We asked the crows where you might be found, and they showed us," Siril replied quietly.

Otto was furious. "You actually brought them here?" he shouted at the crows.

"Well, you see, Sir," one of the crows who had been flying alongside them explained, "they told us they were merchants and that they wanted to do a trade with you. And we thought you would be extremely interested in the goods they had to offer."

"Merchants?" muttered Otto incredulously. He turned to Siril. "And what are you trading in?"

"Words," replied Siril firmly. "And these two here," he indicated Aditi and Beautiful, "are our associates. If you'll just wait, we'll prepare our wares and show them to you."

Otto glared at Aditi. "Are you friends or associates?" he asked angrily.

"Both," Aditi replied.

Otto hesitated. He glared at Siril suspiciously, but he was curious about their wares.

"All right," Otto muttered. "But don't try any tricks."

Siril set to work at once. Otto stood some distance away watching their every move. By now several more crows had appeared. They were perched on the branches of a nearby hibiscus bush. They too were waiting expectantly. It was clear they were hoping for handouts. Siril looked around. There was no sign of Goldie. He wished there had been time to go and fetch Monkeyji. She seemed to know what sort of power Otto wielded. What had she said? As soon as Otto exercised his power, she would become aware of the burst of energy, and she and Opal would be able to find him easily. But how make Otto exercise his power without actually letting him do any harm?

Siril beckoned to Aditi and Beautiful and whispered to them, "Take the two pouches off Gardy's neck, and put a little of the Grow-Large ointment on them from your knapsack."

They did what Siril instructed them to do and soon the two pouches were as large as sacks and the little silver balls consisting of the word-hoard were the size of cannon balls."

"Right," Siril said, "now let's try to deal with Otto. But remember, don't use any words that he might be able to snatch in order to destroy us."

"What sorts of words?" Gardy asked.

"Anything to do with any of us," Aditi told him.

"Like 'lion'? Or 'cub'?" Gardy asked in a low voice.

"Shsh," Beautiful hushed him and gave him a little whack with her trunk. "We've got to be careful. I told him my name, but luckily he didn't believe me. I've learnt my lesson."

"I wish Monkeyji and Opal would come," mumbled Gardy. "I think Monkeyji knows how to deal with him."

Beautiful whacked him once again in order to remind him not to say anyone's name, however softly.

Aditi looked at Siril and the others. "The problem is we'll have to make him exercise his power in order to let M know where he is. We'll have to be careful."

"Right," Siril called to Otto. "Our wares are contained in these sacks." He let Otto have a glimpse of the silver balls.

"Now show us what you've got so that we'll know whether it's worthwhile doing a trade with you."

Otto rummaged in his pockets. They could hear the words he had snatched clinking against each other. Aditi and Siril were becoming increasingly nervous. Would Otto be willing to exchange his snatched words for rolled up balls of silver paper with words written inside them? What would happen when he found out that they didn't really have anything much?

Meanwhile, the crows were getting increasingly excited. "Hey Otto," they cawed. "O King Otto, throw us a word. Come on, throw us a word. What about our commission? Come on, just a juicy little titbit, a nice long word."

Otto turned on the crows. "If you don't shut up, I'll abolish crows."

The crows knew that Otto couldn't actually snatch a word until someone said the word aloud. They weren't too frightened. "Aw, come on, Otto," they persisted, "just throw us a word, maybe two or three words."

"Shut up!" Otto roared. "If you don't shut up, I'll abolish cawing." That worked. The crows kept quiet.

"Now," Otto turned to Siril. Hoping to trick him, he said to him in a matter of fact way, "I don't do business with anyone unless I know his name first."

"Where we come from," Gardy told him, "it's not our custom to use names."

"How do you call each other then?" Otto demanded.

"We use titles," Beautiful told him.

"And what's his title?" Otto wanted to know, pointing at Siril.

"Curator of Circumlocutions," Aditi replied sweetly.

Otto looked at her disbelievingly, but the crows had set up a racket again. "Yeah, snatch that one, Otto — circum-something. Yeah, at least that's a long one."

While they were cawing, Beautiful whispered to Aditi, "What does it mean?"

"Keeper of saying things in a roundabout way," Aditi whispered back. "What we have to do if we don't want him to snatch certain words."

Otto had fixed the crows with a cold stare. "Do you want to lose your voices forever?" he asked.

The crows grew quiet once again.

He turned to Siril. "Okay, show me a word."

Siril pointed to a middle-sized ball, which he was fairly sure contained the word 'arthritis'. He had got it from Monkeyji. If Otto snatched 'arthritis', perhaps it wouldn't

matter. It seemed to be something that sometimes gave Monkeyji a lot of pain. "ARTHRITIS," he said hopefully, looking at Otto.

Otto stretched out his hand for the silver ball, but the crows had started up again. "No, no," they were cawing, "not 'arthritis'. Get a fat, juicy word."

Siril looked at the crows in surprise. "What's wrong with 'arthritis'?" he asked. "It's a perfectly good word."

"We don't care if a word is good or bad. We don't care if it's long or short. We don't care if it's old or new. We don't care if it's dirty or clean. We just like juicy words," the crows rapped. They thought they sounded good, and rapped it out all over again.

"And what is a juicy word?" Siril inquired.

"A word that wriggles and squirms. A word that's got life in it," the crows told him.

Otto ignored the crows, and Aditi picked up the silver ball Siril had indicated and gave it to Otto.

Otto opened up the silver ball and looked inside. He found the word 'arthritis' written on it. For a moment Otto did nothing. Then he crumpled up the silver ball and flung it at Aditi.

"You rotten little cheats!" he shouted. "You're not merchants at all, you're a set of con artists!"

6

The Battle of the Silver Balls

"We are not cheats, you silly boy!" Beautiful yelled back. "We came here to help you."

But Otto was busy shouting at the crows. "Look what you've done, you stupid birds. Couldn't you see that they were lying to you? Now they'll just make trouble for us."

"We're very sorry, King Otto," the crows mumbled. "We thought they would have a storehouse of delicious words."

"What are you going to do to make up for it?" Otto demanded.

"Whatever you tell us to do," the crows said obediently.

"Well, chase them out of here. Fly at them in formation and make them leave," Otto told them.

"You want us to attack them?" the crows asked uncertainly.

"Yesss!" shouted Otto.

As the crows sat on their hibiscus bush and shifted from foot to foot trying to summon up the nerve to attack an elephant, however small, and a lion cub, Goldie and the green dragons wandered back into the courtyard.

"Oh, hello," Goldie said to Beautiful and Aditi, "you look familiar, but as I don't really know who I am, I can't be sure of who you are and who I know and who I don't know, if you see what I mean."

Beautiful and Aditi stared back at Goldie. "Yes, you look familiar to us too," Aditi said to him. "What's your name?"

"That's just it," Goldie told her. "I don't know. These two young fellows here say I'm the tenth dragon." Goldie indicated the two green dragons. "But so what? I could just as easily be the hundredth dragon or the thousandth dragon."

"No, no, no." One of the two green dragons stepped forward. "We're sure he is the Tenth Dragon. He has long been awaited in the city of Hong Kong. The only trouble is he doesn't seem to know who he is. Would you mind keeping an eye on him, while we go away and get help for him?"

"I think we might be in the middle of a battle here, but if you tell him to go and sit down under that frangipani tree over there, we'll do our best to look after him," Aditi said to the green dragons.

As Goldie moved away Aditi and the others could see Otto shouting at the crows. "Attack!" he screamed. "Oh you good for nothing birds! Fly in formation and attack right now!"

Slowly and reluctantly the crows rose in the air and started coming at Beautiful and the others. Gardy immediately picked out a particularly large ball and rolled it towards Beautiful. "PALINDROME, I think. Hurl it, Beautiful!"

Beautiful swung back her trunk and threw the silver ball. The crow formation scattered.

"What does it mean?" Beautiful asked.

"A word that can be spelt both forwards and backwards, like 'Otto'," Siril told her. "Watch out, here they come again." He pointed to another large ball. "LACHRYMOSE, I think. It means 'tearful'."

Beautiful swung it at the crows shouting, "I'll make them lachrymose!" and broke up their formation again.

But the crows re-formed and Gardy pushed another large

ball towards Aditi, "ICHTHYOSAURUS, meaning 'fish dinosaur'. One of my favourites."

Aditi threw it at the oncoming crows and once again the crows scattered.

As the crows re-formed, Beautiful put down the ball she was carrying and charged the crows herself. The crows flew high into the air and eventually settled on the rooftop of the school. Beautiful, meanwhile, continued her charge and uprooted the bush they had been sitting upon.

"Come back , you cowardly crows," Otto shouted to the birds on the rooftop.

"We'll help you from here," the crows shouted back.

"All right," Otto told them. "Just say the word ELEPHANT loudly and clearly. I'll snatch the word out of the air, and then all the elephants in the world will forget who or what they are or ever were."

But before the crows could utter the first syllable, Aditi had raced over to Goldie and asked him to blow the crows right off the rooftop.

"All right," Goldie agreed. "I think you're a friend, though I can't quite remember who you are, or indeed, who I am, for that matter. "

He stood up and breathed out with the strength of a force nine gale. The crows were blown backwards up the roof and some of the tiles on the roof fell off.

"Was that okay?" asked Goldie.

"That was splendid," Aditi told him. "Thanks very much,

whoever you are." She looked hard at him. She felt he was a friend, but though she tried she just couldn't remember who he was. She returned to the battle.

"Oh you useless crows!" Otto was yelling at the crows again. "All you have to do is say three simple syllables. Can't you do that? Come on. Crow No. 1, just say, 'EL'. Crow No. 2, say, 'E,' and Crow No. 3 say, 'PHANT.'"

Crow No. 1 managed to say the first syllable. "EL," she cawed. And before Goldie could blow the crows skywards again, Otto snatched the syllable out of the air. But as Otto raised his hand to snatch the second syllable, Gardy charged him, and knocked him down. The two wrestled on the ground with Siril still clinging to Gardy's ear and cheering him on. Above their heads Crow No. 2 was cawing, "E, E," and Crow No. 3 was shouting "PHANT, PHANT". The other crows were making little dives at Aditi and Beautiful, who were defending themselves with silver balls

"Here's SOMNABULISM for you!" Beautiful cried as she hurled a silver ball at a passing crow.

"And here's IGNOMINIOUS!" Aditi shouted as she hurled another silver ball.

Goldie meanwhile breathed in a hundred silver balls and breathed them out at the crows in a wing formation.

As this commotion was going on Opal and Monkeyji suddenly arrived. The burst of mental energy from Otto when he snatched the syllable 'EL', had been enough to allow Monkeyji to locate him, and Opal had flown her to the school right away. Monkeyji fixed them all in the beam of her one grey eye and commanded them to stop. They did stop. The crows fluttered to the ground. Goldie curled up again under his tree, and Gardy and Otto disengaged and dusted themselves off. Gardy made sure Siril was all right, and set him down on Aditi's shoulder. Then they all looked up at Monkeyji, who was still seated on Opal's back.

7

Monkeyji to the Rescue

Monkeyji surveyed the battlefield with a dispassionate eye. The ground was littered with silver balls. The hibiscus bush Beautiful had uprooted was lying on the ground with its roots in the air, and there were broken tiles scattered all over the courtyard.

A beam of grey light shot from Monkeyji's eye and enclosed Otto. As the others watched, Otto rose three feet into the air and was turned upside down. Then he was given a little shaking so that everything in his pockets fell out. Monkeyji motioned to Aditi to gather up the contents of his pockets.

Aditi picked up everything carefully and put it all in a clean cotton handkerchief. His pockets contained about two dozen words. They waited to see what would happen next.

"You're a very irresponsible boy," Monkeyji said. "What were you proposing to do with these words?"

"I don't know," mumbled Otto. "Anyway, it's none of your business."

"It certainly is my business," Monkeyji told him.

"Why? Who do you think you are?" Otto answered rudely.

At this Gardy sprang to Monkeyji's defence. "Don't you dare speak to Monkeyji like that. If you do, I'll head-butt you," he told Otto.

As soon as Gardy uttered the word MONKEYJI, Otto's right hand flew up and he commanded his brain to snatch the word. Nothing happened. Otto's hand stayed raised in the air and he found that he couldn't move at all. Once again he was enclosed in the cold light of Monkeyji's eye. Gardy looked at him and laughed, "You look like a traffic policeman, only there isn't any traffic to stop." Otto didn't say anything at all; he couldn't.

"Now then, Otto," Monkeyji said to the frozen boy, "we did, in fact, come here to help you, not to harm you. If I release you, you will have to behave yourself. Tell me, what were you planning to do with the words you snatched?"

Monkeyji had released Otto, and the boy now mumbled. "I only gave the crows a couple of really nasty words the boys kept calling me. I wasn't going to feed these to the crows. They're mostly the names of the boys and some masters."

When the crows heard that Otto hadn't intended to give them anymore words to eat, they set up a tremendous cawing, and a few of them began to dive at Otto. Gardy came to his rescue and jumped at the crows to drive them away. And Aditi and Beautiful helped as well by chucking a few silver balls at the crows.

Monkeyji watched the crows being driven away. She looked at Otto. "Can't say you deserved their help against the crows."

"No. Perhaps I didn't. But I couldn't very well defend myself, could I? You've taken away my powers," Otto retorted.

"Oh don't be silly, Otto," Siril snapped from Aditi's shoulder. "You've seen the power Monkeyji has, and she's said we're here to help you. Why don't you learn from her instead of trying to fight her. We're not your enemies, we're your friends."

"I don't have any friends!" Otto answered sulkily.

"Well, it's about time you learnt to make some," Siril retorted. He was losing patience. High overhead he could see that the crows were gathering again. He was beginning to think that Otto really wasn't worth helping even though Grendel had asked them to help him.

Otto glared at Siril, "Do you want to be my friend?"

"Well, I don't want to be your enemy," Siril answered.

"And what about you?" Otto glared at Beautiful.

Beautiful shifted from foot to foot. "Well, I don't know," she mumbled. "You really have been awful. But I don't want to hurt you."

Gardy began to feel sorry for Otto. He could see that nobody wanted to be his friend much. "I'll be your friend," he offered. "I'm always being accused of being too bumptious and too friendly, and you're clearly not much good at making friends, so we'll probably correct each other."

Otto stared at Gardy in astonishment. "You mean you're willing to be my friend? Even after we fought each other?"

Gardy shrugged. "Why not? Friends fight. Come on, let's have a game of Multi-Football."

"No, wait," Otto restrained him. "I think there are one or two things I ought to do first." Otto turned to Monkeyji. "Please," he said. "the truth is I don't know how to release all these words I've snatched. I'm sorry to have caused so much trouble. I didn't know what to do. Some of the boys really were making my life miserable."

"I'll show you what to do," Monkeyji told him. She asked Aditi to put the handkerchief on the ground and to place the words at some distance from each other.

"They're like little dodecahedrons," Siril murmured.

Gardy overheard him. "DODECAHEDRON! Wow! I'll store that in my word-hoard." Looking at the silver balls lying on the ground, he added, "If I can ever gather it up again."

"Now, choose a word and warm it gently by concentrating on it," Monkeyji told Otto.

Aditi pointed to a word that looked more golden and slightly different from the others. "Here, do this one first," she suggested. She didn't know why, but she felt that that one was important.

Otto concentrated on the golden word, and gradually it began to melt and then suddenly, with a little puff, it vanished into the air.

"What happened to it?" Beautiful asked.

"It's gone back into circulation again," Monkeyji told her.

Everyone had been busy watching Otto concentrate. They hadn't noticed that the crows had ranged themselves for another attack. The sight of the words spread out like that in front of them had been too much for them. As the crows attacked, Goldie lumbered out from beneath the frangipani tree. When he saw what the crows were doing, he drew in his breath and let it out again in a strong gust so that the crows were knocked sideways. But then another strong gust hit them from the other side and blew them towards Goldie again.

It was Opal doing exactly what Goldie had done, but this time Goldie held his breath and let the crows fly away.

8

Otto and Gardy

Everyone greeted Goldie joyfully. "Where have you been?" they asked.

"I'm not quite sure," Goldie answered. He spied Otto. "The last thing I remember clearly is telling this boy my name."

"He must have snatched it!" Beautiful exclaimed.

Upon hearing this, Goldie seized Otto in one of his claws and held him up high in the air so that they were now face to face. Otto was terrified. The effect of the Grow-Small ointment was wearing off, and Goldie and Opal, and Beautiful as well, were returning to their full size. Meanwhile the silver balls, which had been the size of cannon balls were shrinking into little pellets again. Gardy could see that Otto was frightened to death. He jumped on Goldie's back and climbed up to his head.

"Don't worry, Otto," he called to his new friend. "Goldie might be cross with you, but he won't hurt you. He never does. Just say you're sorry."

"I'm very sorry, Sir," Otto managed to say.

"All right," Goldie growled, "but don't go around snatching words. You've got to undo the harm you've done."

He set Otto down, and with Monkeyji's help they released the remaining words. It was getting dark, and they decided that Monkeyji and the others would return to the boat for the night.

"What about me?' wondered Otto. 'What will happen to me as the schoolmasters and the boys begin remembering who they are?" He didn't say anything aloud, but Gardy guessed his thoughts.

"It's all right, old fellow, I'll stay with you for a day or two until things are properly settled," he told Otto. "I can, can't I?" he asked the others.

Siril and Monkeyji consulted.

"That's not a bad idea," Siril agreed. "We'll meet you here at sunrise tomorrow before the rest of the school is up."

Aditi and Gardy gathered up the silver pellets as best as they could and returned them to the little pouches. Aditi looked at Gardy anxiously. Would the cub be able to manage? She took the cloak of invisibility out of the howdah, packed it tightly in a small bag and tied the bag around Gardy's neck. "Just in case," she said. "You never know."

"An excellent idea," Siril applauded. "Do you want my magic clay as well?"

But to this offer, the cub said, "No, thank you. I'm not adept at using it in the way you are. Don't worry about us. We'll be fine. What shall we tell the green dragons if they return?"

"Tell them to meet us here tomorrow morning," Goldie replied. Then Siril settled himself on Aditi's shoulder and Aditi and Monkeyji climbed onto Opal's back, while Goldie picked up Beautiful carefully and flew with her.

Otto and Gardy waved to them and turned to go into the school buildings.

"I say, what's Multi-Football?" Otto asked.

"Oh, it's when you play football with twenty-two balls and only two players," Gardy replied.

"You made that up," Otto accused him.

Goldie shrugged. "It's possible to make new words as well as snatch them," he replied.

"True," Otto replied thoughtfully. "Come on, let's go and play Four-Dimensional Chess."

"I can't even play two-dimensional chess properly never mind three-dimensional. And as for four-dimensional chess, I've never heard of it!"

"I made it up," Otto told him.

"How do you play it?" Gardy demanded.

"It's easy," Otto replied. "There's a parallel chessboard on which each of the squares stands for a day of the week, beginning with Sunday and ending with Sunday. You move forwards and backwards in time, so that what actually happens is contingent on what may have happened in the past or on what will have happened in the future because of a move you've already made."

"Wow," said Gardy as they went indoors.

At first things were quiet. The crows had flown away and gone home to roost. The befuddled schoolmasters, who were gradually recovering, couldn't work out what had happened to them. They decided that the best thing to do was to send the boys to bed. The boys were also confused, even the ones who hadn't had their names snatched. They couldn't understand why there had been no lessons or why they had been allowed to play all day. They filed into the dormitory quietly and began getting ready for bed. But when Otto and Gardy walked in, the chief bully saw them and couldn't resist getting in a dig at Otto.

"Hey, Otto," the chief bully called, thinking from a distance that Gardy was a toy animal, "what's that stuffed thing you're dragging along? Are you still such a baby that you need a teddy bear?"

A soon as they heard this, the chief bully's two assistant began to chant, "Otto needs a Teddy Bear. Otto needs a Teddy Bear. Otto is a Baby. Otto needs a Teddy." They went on and on.

Otto didn't like being humiliated, especially not in front of his friend, Gardy. He drew himself up and said to the chief bully, "I'm not a baby. You're the ones who are being childish."

But this just infuriated the bullies, and they began throwing pillows at him. Li, one of the other boys in the dormitory, protested to the bully. "Hey, leave Otto alone. He isn't hurting you."

"That's a possible ally," Gardy whispered to Otto.

The chief bully turned on Li. He didn't want anyone questioning him. "Are you going to stand up for our Baby here? You'll have to fight me if you are, because you see, I don't like boys who behave like babies."

The bully's assistants got on either side of Li and began to push him around.

"Come on," Gardy said to Otto. "We've got to help him. He stood up for us."

Otto and Gardy ran to Li's aid, and before anyone realised what was happening, Gardy had bitten the ankle of each of the bully's two helpers. They began hopping about and crying loudly.

"What's the matter with you?" Otto mocked them. "Did you get bitten by a teddy bear?"

Several other boys had joined them now. They were tired of having their lives made miserable by the chief bully and his two assistants and were glad to see that someone was standing up to them at last. The chief bully had to establish that he was still the boss. He waded in with the firm intention of knocking down Li and Otto. He hadn't seen Gardy properly yet as Gardy was still underfoot. Otto and Li stood their ground even though the bully was a couple of years older and much larger than them. But before the bully could hit them, Gardy took a flying

leap and head-butted the bully full in the chest. The chief bully let out a terrified squawk and fell to the ground.

Otto and Li with the help of several boys proceeded to tie up the hands of the bully and his two assistants with dressing gown cords. They lined them up against the wall.

Otto spoke to them severely, "You must promise faithfully that you will never attempt to bully any of us again."

"We promise," mumbled the chief bully.

"Do you know what will happen if you break your promise?" Li asked them.

"No," mumbled the assistants.

"All of us will jump on you and tie you up all over again," Li told him.

"Yes!" roared the other boys. "Yes! We will!"

"We promise," the bully and his assistants mumbled. "We promise never to bully anyone again."

The boys untied them. Li and Otto shook hands. Otto thanked Li for standing up for him, and Li patted his shoulder and said, "Anytime, mate." Then Otto looked around for Gardy. He was about to search for Gardy, when he noticed a lump under the top blanket at the foot of his bed. He got into bed, bent over and whispered "Thanks". And in no time at all, Otto, like Gardy, was fast asleep.

9

The Unexpected One

Gardy woke up just before sunrise. He scampered up to the head of the bed and shook Otto by the shoulder. "Come on, wake up. It's nearly sunrise. We've got to meet the others."

Otto woke up quickly and threw on his dressing gown. He and Goldie went out into the courtyard. They found the two green dragons scurrying about and looking in every possible hiding place (as well as a great many impossible ones) in the hope of finding Goldie.

Gardy went up to them and said, "You're looking for Goldie, aren't you?"

"We are looking for the Revered Tenth Dragon, Sir," one of the green dragons told him. "Do you know where he might be?"

"Don't know about the Tenth Dragon," Gardy replied, "but if you wait for a minute or two, Goldie and the others will soon be here."

As he spoke Opal and Goldie appeared overhead and soon landed in the courtyard. The four adventurers climbed out of the howdah and came towards Otto.

"Well?" Monkeyji said to Gardy and Otto. How did you get on?"

Gardy considered whether he ought to lie to Monkeyji. He didn't know whether getting into a fight was all right.

"Well," he began cautiously. "The cloak of invisibility was jolly useful. We just covered ourselves up in it and then they couldn't find us and so they couldn't bully us."

"No, no, he's being modest," Otto interrupted hurriedly. "That's not what happened at all. A chap called Li stood up for us, and Gardy bit the bully's assistants in the ankles. And – "

Siril looked at Gardy. "You bit the bully's assistants?" he asked. "I thought you had given up biting."

"I had. I have. But they were about to bash Otto and Li," Gardy told him.

"Ah well, that's different," murmured Siril.

"And then what happened?" asked Aditi.

"Then the bully waded in and Gardy took a flying leap and head-butted him," Otto went on.

"Head-butting's allowed, isn't it?" asked Gardy anxiously.

"Definitely, under the circumstances," Monkeyji told him.

"And then," Otto continued, "we tied up the bullies and

Li and I made them promise never to bully any of us again."

"Who's Li?" Beautiful asked.

"Otto's made a good friend," Gardy told the others.

"Yes, but you were my first good friend," Otto told him. He turned to the others. "You should have seen Gardy! He was the hero. When the fight was over, all the boys were looking for him, but he had fallen asleep at the foot of my bed. He looked so tired, I let him sleep."

"So you didn't get lionised?" Aditi teased.

"What's 'lionised'?" asked Gardy.

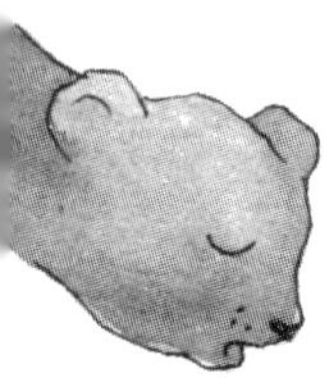

"Being treated like a lion, like somebody important," Aditi replied.

The lion cub shook his head. "I just wanted to help Otto," he said simply.

"You're a good chap," Siril told him.

"Will you be all right now?" Opal asked Otto.

"I think so," Otto replied uncertainly.

"You sound uncertain," Monkeyji said gently. "Haven't you understood your real power?"

"What real power? " Otto asked.

Gardy nudged him. "Making new words, not snatching them," Gardy whispered.

"What are new words?" Otto asked.

Monkeyji shrugged, "New ideas."

"Like the theory of evolution," Aditi offered.

"Or the theory of relativity," Siril put in.

"Or a new game," Gardy added.

"Or a new name," Goldie said.

"Or a new sound," Opal chimed in.

"I see," Otto replied. "Yes, I begin to see."

Meanwhile the two green dragons had sidled closer. They gazed up at Goldie. "Please Sir, you are now more than twice the size you were when we saw you last. Nevertheless, we are convinced you are the Tenth Dragon. A delegation of dragons will arrive any moment now. When the Keeper of the Scrolls reads from the ancient prophecy we will know at once whether or not you are indeed the Awaited One."

Goldie didn't have a chance to reply. Five more dragons appeared in the sky, three red ones, one large green one and one white one holding a scroll.

They landed and the large green dragon addressed Goldie, "O Noble Tenth Dragon, we want you to be our king, please."

"No," said Goldie. "I'm not royal or anything like that, and I don't want to be anybody's ruler."

"He declines," shouted the white dragon. "It's written here. We will offer him the crown and he will decline it. He is, indeed the Tenth Dragon."

The large green dragon bowed to Goldie, "Sir, even if you do not agree to be our king, will you and your friends and any other guests you choose to invite at least attend the dragon celebration to be held on the bay in your honour this evening?"

"Of course," replied Goldie. "It is very kind of you to ask us. I will be delighted to attend as will all our friends here."

Goldie bent his head to speak to Otto, "You're invited too. Bring Li and any of the other boys you want to bring. Gardy and I will come to fetch you. Make sure you ask permission first. Just ask politely and they'll give it to you."

"Great!" shouted Gardy.

The seven dragons were about to leave, when suddenly they caught sight of Opal. They stopped in their tracks as though thunderstruck.

"Who is she?" muttered the large green dragon.

"There is no prophecy about the Eleventh Dragon," moaned the white dragon.

Otto glanced at Monkeyji, and when she seemed to approve, he stepped forward. "The beautiful dragon is Opal," he told them. "She is called The Unexpected One."

All the dragons bowed and cried out, "Hail to The Unexpected One. You honour us with your presence." The title had made sense to them. Then they took their leave and flew away to make arrangements for the evening's celebrations. Monkeyji nodded imperceptibly in Otto's direction; and Otto raised his hand imperceptibly and saluted her.

Just as the adventurers were about to leave, a thornless rose fell out of the sky. It righted itself and stood upright in front of Monkeyji.

"A digital rose!" Siril exclaimed.

In Grendel's voice it uttered two words, "Thanks, everybody." Then it bowed deeply from the stem downwards and vanished.

The four adventurers got into the howdah. Everyone called, "Goodbye for now. See you this evening." Suddenly Beautiful scrambled out of the howdah with a small sack of peanuts held in her trunk. She set it down beside Otto.

"For the crows," she whispered, "just in case they need it."

Aditi and her friends find the Word Eater in Hong Kong . . .

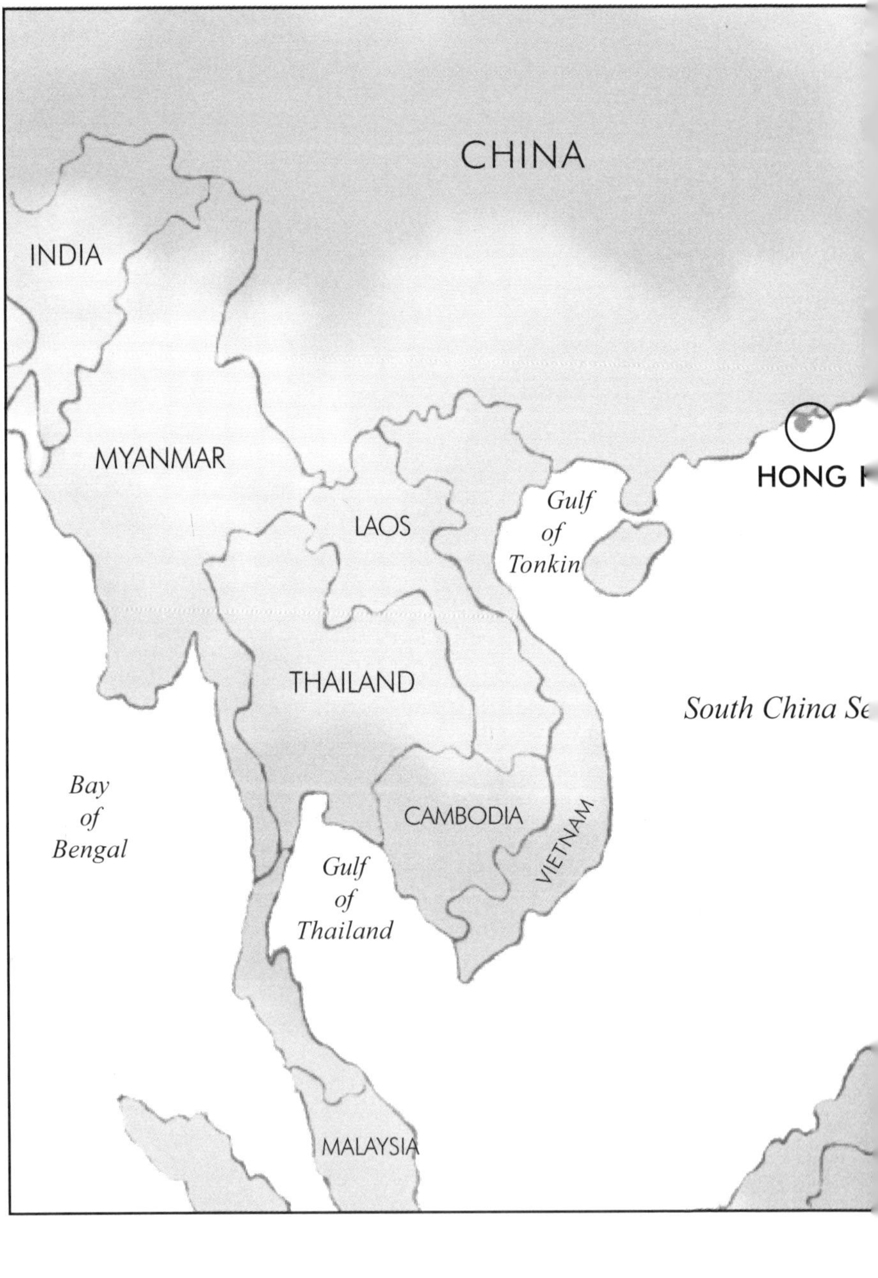

. . . the city of dragons

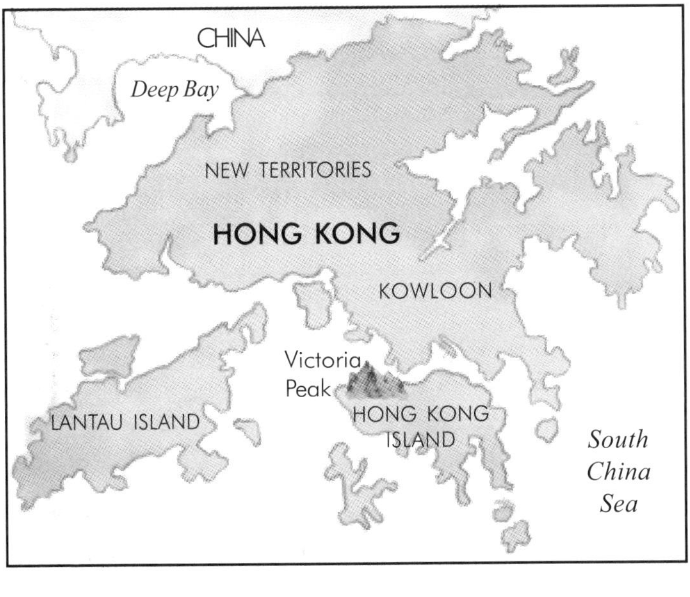

THE ADITI ADVENTURE PACKS

UNLIKELY FRIENDS

Aditi and the One-eyed Monkey
Aditi and the Thames Dragon
Aditi and the Marine Sage
Aditi and the Techno Sage

In the first set of adventures, Aditi, Monkeyji, Siril the ant and Beautiful Ele the Beautiful Elephant make friends with the two dragons, Goldie and Opal, and are helped by The Three Sages and help them in turn. The challenges they face are not just a matter of fighting an enemy with whatever skill and ingenuity they have. They also have to think about various questions. What is the best way to deal with someone unreasonable who is stronger than you? What is the difference between a real dragon and an unreal dragon? Is solving a set of problems without actually fighting anyone also an adventure? What happens to someone who can remember what happened, but not the order in which it happened?

If you are a person who likes asking questions, then these are books you'll enjoy.

UNEXPECTED MONSTERS

Aditi and her Friends take on the Vesuvian Giant
Aditi and her Friends meet Grendel
Aditi and her Friends help the Budapest Changeling
Aditi and her Friends in search of Shemeek

In In the second set of adventures, Aditi and the others encounter various figures from myth and legend from different parts of Europe who behave in unexpected and sometimes alarming ways. The Sybil of Cumae turns out to be helpful. Grendel the monster is only a boy; he forgets every day whatever it was that happened the day before. The Budapest Changeling changes in accordance with how she's perceived. And the white horse of Wysherad, the wise Shemeek, has to help Monkeyji who has had a spell cast on her so that

she's unable to speak without telling a lie. Questions arise: what is strength? Does knowing yourself matter? Does who you are depend on who you've been? Does it also depend on how others see you? Can you communicate anything if you have to lie? The four adventurers and the two dragons rise to the challenge and become better friends than ever.

If you like thinking about things, you'll relish these adventures.

HEROES

Gardy in the City of Lions
Monkeyji and the Word Eater
Siril and the Spaceflower
Beautiful and the Cyberspace Runaway

In the third set of adventures, one or another of the friends is central and the others get embroiled. For example, Siril the ant falls in love or appears to fall in love, and they all find themselves setting off on a voyage to one of the moons of Jupiter. Or Beautiful Ele the Beautiful Elephant decides that she is going to turn into a rational elephant, but then finds that she and the others have to do some very peculiar things in order to help that most rational of creatures, Mistress i, who was born in a computer. There's also an adventure in which Monkeyji comes to the fore as she wields her mental powers with the skill and panache of a true hero. Gardy gets into difficulties when a distant relative asks him to help deal with a problem without realising that he is the problem, or at least a part of it. Questions arise. Is being rational always good? Are impossible friendships sometimes possible? If a word disappears, does that mean that for all practical purposes, the thing itself also disappears? What is seeing clearly about – guessing the future, seeing how things are or seeing how they should be?

If you like to mix your admiration with an occasional smile, then these heroic deeds will entertain you.

Other paperbacks from Tulika

Andamans Boy
That Summer at Kalagarh
Journey to the City of Six Gates
Just a Train Ride Away
The Smile of Vanuvati
Kabir the Weaver-Poet
The Forbidden Temple: stories from the past
Sorry, Best Friend!
One World
Parthiban's Dream
Pippi Lambemoze (Hindi)

forthcoming

Animalwrites: blogposts on wildlife in India
The Runaway Auto
Rini's Story